Solace in Stanza

Priyanka Dhruv

BookLeaf Publishing

India | USA | UK

Presentation by *BookLeaf Publishing*

Web: www.bookleafpub.com

E-mail: info@bookleafpub.com

ISBN: 9789360946470

First edition 2024

ACKNOWLEDGEMENT

The completion of "Solace in Stanza" has been a journey marked by countless moments of inspiration, encouragement, and support. As I reflect on the creation of this collection, I am filled with gratitude to Shiva & Shakti, my inner guiding light, always helping me traverse through experiences and create art from the same. I am grateful for their manifestations in all my Gurus, speaking through me in reality and my meditations.

I am immensely thankful to Mom, Dad, and my extended family filled with all those who have given their unwavering support and belief in my writing journey. Their encouragement has been a constant source of strength and inspiration, and I am forever grateful for their love and encouragement.

To my friends, my cheerleaders, and unpaid therapists.

I would also like to thank the team at BookLeaf Publishing, whose '21-Day Writing Challenge' has made the publication of "Solace in Stanza" a reality. I am honoured to have had the opportunity to work with you.

And lastly, my gratitude goes out to our dear friend, Late Mr. Dominique Lapierre, whose life philosophy guides mine, Tanashtam Yanna Diyate, meaning 'all that is not given, is lost.'

With heartfelt appreciation,

Priyanka Dhruv

PREFACE

In the labyrinthine alleys of Mumbai, amidst the cacophony of its streets and the kaleidoscope of its cultures, I dream, I envision and I write—a collection of poetry.

As I sit down to pen these words, I am filled with a sense of gratitude and humility, for the journey that has led me to this moment. Born from a desire to explore the intersection of art and life, "Solace in Stanza" is the culmination of years of introspection, observation, and creative expression.

In these pages, you will find each poem, a reflection of a moment in time, a snapshot of a memory, an imagination, as seen through the eyes of a poet navigating the complexities of existence. It is a journey, both for the reader and for the writer.

In crafting these poems, I have drawn inspiration from experiences that have shaped me. But above all, I have drawn inspiration from the act of writing itself—from the joy of stringing together words like pearls on a necklace, from the solace found in the rhythm of verse. I hope my hand-drawn illustrations convey each poem's essence to the reader.

As you embark on this journey, I invite you to open your mind and your soul to the beauty contained within these pages. May these poems serve as a beacon of light in the darkness, a source of comfort in times of sorrow, and a reminder that, no matter how far we may stray from the path, solace can always be found in the stanza.

With gratitude,
Priyanka Dhruv

Perfect Imperfections

I am no longer afraid.
Afraid of heartbreaks, of any sort.
I am no longer afraid,
Cause fear,
Isn't a feeling that deserves a home,
A soft blanket,
A plate of comfort food,
Even a casket,
Cause fear,
Isn't a feeling that deserves our time,
And time is precious.
I don't want to entangle my present.
My present is precious,
My present is gold,
It's everything a textbook,
Ever told.
Am I being unrealistic?
Dreamy?
Too philosophical, maybe?
But I am a poet,
I don't let my pen compromise with this ink
gushing out of my heart.
In fact,
If there is any fear whatsoever,
Creeping,
Isolating,

Negating,
Even a milligram of positive thought,
I let my paper absorb it,
To the point that it drips of the very same ink.
Blurring all the words for me,
To no longer,
See them,
Read them,
Feel them,
Instead,
Just heal.
My heart now,
Is Wabi-Sabi,
A Japanese philosophy.
My heart isn't a bright red,
Spotless,
Gleaming,
Beaming,
Perfect curves,
Constantly beating.
My heart is,
Noir,
Sepia,
Chrome,
Even a burst of colour sometimes.
My heart has,
Cracks,
Bruises,
And Scars,

Ever so often,
Skipping a beat,
Taking a retreat,
Perfectly Imperfect,
Wabi-Sabi.
I am no longer afraid,
Cause there isn't a thing,
Ever made,
More powerful than a heart,
All sewed up,
With the threads of thoughts,
Held by the needle,
Of unconditional self-love.

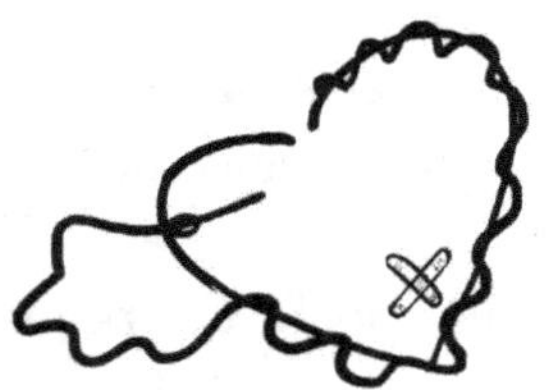

Dear Soulmate

In an ocean of many beating hearts,
Each manufacturing a giant wave coming your
way,
Would you find mine?
Will the rhythm of my beats match the
frequency of yours?
I know it would.

You could not be more different than me.
We have shared similar traumas and heartaches.
Even though our stories are different,
The moments we lived through them,
Resemble at their core.
A heart in pain,
Through not just tears, mood swings, anger, or
disdain,
Is a heart, after all.
The pain, in its most natural manifestation,
Would not feel any different from another soul.

Your journey lifts mine.
I have seen you in a time that has not even come
yet.
I have seen you when I am most at peace within
myself.
You appear right across from me,

Visit there, speak,
Hold my hand and smile.
You soothe my anxiety,
You let my restless cells,
Hold still.
Do you see me in your visions too?

There is so much love to give,
A million stories we could share,
At bedtime and more.
We have worlds to conquer,
And universes to create.
Our sanctuary of goodness and healing,
Where we learn and teach each other,
Absolving our insecurities,
And securing our virtues.

Debating on the things that matter,
And sometimes, the ones that don't,
I would argue playfully.
You are just like me,
Vocalising monologues, connecting dots,
Proving your point.
I would be quiet,
Let you finish speaking,
My fake frown,
Would not hold any longer,
And as I would break into a smile,
You would realise,

Pull me close, kiss me, and quiet the room.
As words would cease,
The sounds of our breath would be the only
ones,
Filling up the room.

As the sun rises from the ocean bed and lights
up the sky,
I want his guiding light to help you spot me.
I am right here,
Being vulnerable,
In my heart's case, unboxing myself to you.
I wasn't ready for this,
But now it's time.

Revisiting Fairy Tales

There is something almost magical about 12 am,
As the night shifts into a deeper night,
And the skies fill with starry lights.

Cinderella transforms back.
I wonder why it was only the glass slipper,
That did not vanish,
Stayed intact,
Never turned back to magic dust!

Was there a parallel version,
Somewhere in a different dimension,
One in which,
Cinderella stood on the steps of the castle,
Dancing away with the Crown Prince,
Much until midnight and beyond.
She too,
Just like the glass slipper,
Existed.
Was it about being in the moment,
Away from rules, boundaries, and inhibitions,
Just becoming.

I could feel the midnight stretching on my
tongue,
As the nights eased into the morning Sun.

These fairy tales cross my mind.
Makes me wonder,
What fate would Snow White have,
Had the magic mirror,
Declared the queen fairest of all!
Snow White would have been the Dear
Daughter,
To the mother who wasn't hers and yet her own.

If only Ugly Duckling would have a similar fate,
His miseries and woes,
He would never face.
Since his first breath loved and liked,
For how different he was,
Sad if he were to develop a God-complex!
Becoming a humble Swan.

Pinocchio would never tread from his path to
school,
Losing his mind to sweet talkers,
He met on the road.
The class monitor ensured,
He walked straight to the classroom.
He would discover himself,
Through stories and books,
Honesty, sincerity and bravery,
The virtues he did choose,
Becoming a real boy,
By distinguishing the rights from wrongs,

Not from a journey that ended in a whale's
stomach,
But through other adventures, his destiny
brought.

Messages from a Bookshelf

If the pages of your story start to fray, hope
slowly now turning grey,
Bookmark the page that made your day.

Look for words, that brought a smile to your
face,
The sentences they create, you mentally
embrace.

Look for punctuations that made you pause and
stop,
Remember those tears, and the words that blot.

Look for the threads that bind those pages
strong,
Their rhythm, through the spine, is your journey
far along.

Look for the cover, now weathered with marks,
Don't judge, but reignite your spark.

Look at the pages, yellow, with corners creased,
Smell them, and sigh, have your anxiety
released.

Look for the page with chapters indexed,

Milestones of the journey, the mirrors of
conscience reflect.

Look for the page mentioning
acknowledgments,
Remember, the ones never leaving your side
deserve the compliment.

Reach out to them readers, your cheerleaders,
giving those raving reviews,
Uplifting feelings pursue.

Reread your story, that remained the same,
At its core, which never changed.

A walk to my shore

She walked all the way, to the horizon,
Where the sky kissed land,
With the Sun settling into newer skies,
Merging the day into a velvet night.

The walk was now soothing,
As cold winds brushed past her soft skin.
Her hands turned ice cold.
They always had that tendency.

She missed his warm touch.
They would hold hands,
Intermittently, stealing moments,
And escaping glances from the crowd.

The horizon was still warm with departure.
It was in its essence to be both,
Cold and warm,
Essaying convergence,
Where the opposites settled in peace.

As the velvet night spread to her part of the
world,
She no longer felt darkness.
The night was rich with a thousand shining stars,
Placed in perfect balance.

It was almost as if God had placed each one with
a specific purpose.
The biggest star in the sky then,
Was shining brightly halfway across the world,
Giving its light to someone else.

She was a child born from the wild ocean.
The waves and currents had trained her well.
Seven seas apart wasn't where she would find
her true happiness,
But right here, by the shore, the only heart that
mattered,
Had been waiting all along.

Telepathic Signals

Where do you keep your secrets?
You are out there for the world to see.
You tell those stories with cliffhangers,
Open to interpretation.

Some mornings, you show your face,
Still in bed, occupying just the half of it,
Across a lonely breakfast table,
By the balcony and your trees.

The sunlight cutting through structures,
Forming patterns on your floor.
The rays meet your face,
Eyes shut, you dwell in the warmth.

Hoping for a shadow cooling,
From a familiar face,
Looking down on you,
Whose eyes do you want yours to meet?

Your voice helps me sleep,
The rhythmic breathing,
A lullaby to my lungs.
Can my calm be even calculated?

You help me without you knowing.
Decluttering my mind, one room at a time.
Yesterday was the hallway of self-doubt,
And the day before drawers of restlessness.

I hear your stories,
Poetic expressions,
Read between the lines,
Knowing they are backdated love letters,
Just released.

And I hope one day when we finally meet,
I can tell you I decoded those secrets,
A long time ago,
Your memories and messages,
Still, seek me.

My eyes wish to look,
Into only yours,
Every morning, when they open,
And every night when they close.

Sleepless Nights

I am wide awake in the dead of the night,
Thoughts drifting,
To my mind's delight.
First, before the second,
And a second before the third,
So many in a queue,
Oh, there is no dearth.
Unstoppable now, bearing that overthinker's
curse,
Difficult to contain,
Like arrows of questions shot,
Answers detained.
I look away into the darkness,
Unsure what my mind's eye is waiting to see.
A patch of colour,
On a wall all black?
Oh common! Can you cut me some slack?
Alright, you sleepless night,
What is the purpose of your coming?
12.00 am surprises, 2.00 am regrets, 3.00 am
calls, 4.00 am miracles,
It will be 6.00 am soon,
Can you help me forget?
Twisting and turning,
A workout of sorts,
The gym membership,

I never signed up for!
A marathon my mind's been running,
Burning calories through contemplation.
I scroll through social portals,
Leading to no-good conclusions,
And projections, far from reality.
I pen down those plans,
Attitudinal shifts,
The organiser laughs,
My procrastination is a prick.
Easily soon, I think,
Shall I wander? maybe to places far off,
It is a sleepless night!
Oh! Just take off.
A beach, a mountain,
An island could have both.
A garden, a lake,
The village of which he spoke.
Anime movies rerun,
In my mind's cineplex,
Nature, weather, music and more,
Dance, romance and drama galore.
Just when the climax,
Leads to the end credits,
The alarm bells ring,
My sleepless night,
A blue Monday it brings!

Safekeeping Paper-Thin Hearts

These days,
Love drifts like a feather,
Floating in the summer breeze.
The right swipes,
Those temporary likes.
Those blind voice calls,
Echoing in empty halls.
The whispers so hushed,
The adrenaline rush.
Imaginations running wild,
Like a garden filled with butterflies.
The pressure to please,
Hold a conversation,
Making them ignore,
Every other notification on the screen.
Turning seconds and one-word replies,
Into hours of long chats forming paragraphs.
Undressing each other's minds,
With those conversations,
Even though fully dressed,
Completely naked now,
Through vulnerabilities and anxieties,
Revealed.
We are all really,

Safekeeping paper-thin hearts.
You see,
Creased paper never smooths again.
Our hearts, unlike those sheets,
Unwrinkle from the most tenacious squeeze,
Extracting,
Every ounce of last love that we may have.
Our heart,
A treasury of emotions,
Depleting now,
Treading towards a negative balance,
My heart's safe deposits of Self-love,
Keeping it afloat.
I overdraft,
Because of all the things I call my own,
The one I cannot afford to lose,
Is Hope!
And when it's right,
Those long phone calls,
Eating away their sleep time,
Turns their restless slumber,
Into a tranquil sleep.

I want to go back in time

I want to go back in time,
And feel what sand felt like the first time,
How the ocean breeze felt on my skin,
How I would run towards the water,
Care a damn about anything,
Let the waves kiss my feet, and as they went
back,
Leaving deep imprints in the wet sand.

I want to go back in time,
Travel alone on a plane for the first time,
Choose the window seat,
Stare at the blue skies outside,
Sailing through clouds,
While listening to Rahman.

I want to go back in time and taste Ice Gola for
the first time,
Hear the bells ring on empty streets,
As I would run to Ba and ask for ten rupees,
Ek Kala Khatta dena uncle.
Would sip till I find my peace,
Till the afternoon rays ease.

I want to go back in time,
Look at the starry skies for the first time.

Not a made-up one at the city planetarium,
A real one, from a mountain,
I remember being stunned,
I could not believe my eyes,
For it was beautiful,
Beyond what words could describe.
We made constellations lying on the grass that
night.

I want to go back in time,
And score a basket for the first time,
Dribble a certain length,
Turn the ball slightly backward,
As my hands moved upwards,
Aiming across an imaginary line,
Scoring from quite the distance.

I want to go back in time,
Read 'The Diary of Anne Frank' for the first
time.
My little teenage self,
Making a friend in Anne,
Only imagining,
What a beautiful woman,
She would have grown up to be,
And read pages of her diary,
As she finds hope & love,
In troubling times.

I want to go back in time,
And see the birds at Jurong for the first time.
Grabbing the best seats,
I could not stop smiling as one after the other,
Those winged beauties flew on commands,
As tears strolled down my eyes,
I asked myself,
Have you ever felt extremely happy?
Just by watching birds?
I was overwhelmed.
I think I am a bird inside.

I want to go back in time,
Listen to 'Tu Jhoom' for the very first time,
The goosebumps rose on my skin,
Tears of joy, mind on a spin,
As I translate the song,
Through moments in life,
Where the words hit me like,
Conversations I sought,
From no one but me.

I want to go back in time and play Holi,
At Nathdwara for the first time.
Gulaal on the walls of the haveli and in the air.
Musical instruments echo through the halls,
The atmosphere reverberates with kirtans and
chants,
Krishna Kanhaiya Lal ki Jai,

Aaj ke Anand ki Jai.

I want to go back,
And relive those First Times.

Journaling

It is never too late to rewrite your story,
To turn a new page,
Filling it with all the stories that would be,
Instead of those that have been,
Or, could be.
Living in the past,
Even though seems comforting,
Could not do you any good.
The crisp, fresh pages,
Await your dreams,
Articulated in poetry,
Which only you would know,
To rhyme and recite.
And even if your notebook ends,
And sometimes,
You may feel,
It has been enough,
With mostly scribbles and doodles,
Instead of words,
Which made the difference.
It's fine.
Those scribbled curves,
And mindless drawings,
Led to lines,
Having complete sense,
Not just to you,
But others too.

Meditation

A practice in meditation,
Seeking that divine,
Towards the truth inclined.
Climbing those mountains,
Reaching those heights,
Trekking over hills,
Illusions clarified.

Patches of colour,
Bursting through the darkness,
A tunnel leading to the light.
My breath moving,
Upwards and downwards,
My centres energised.

In Silence,
Conversing the most.
Questions and Answers,
With passing thoughts.

Seconds to minutes,
And minutes to hours.
The concept of time,
My heart devours.

Listening more than I speak,
Seeking more than I ask.
Surrendering to the universe,
Surrendering at last.

Breakfast at Matunga

In a quaint neighbourhood,
Slowly losing it's old world charm,
Exists,
My filter coffee memory.
The aroma of the beans,
At a breakfast table,
Shared with strangers,
Us lurking over dishes,
Others ordered,
Exchanging odd glances.
Smiling infectiously,
We aren't strangers anymore.
The waiters, running,
Mind faster than their feet,
Memorising one idli, two dosa,
Was it wada dipped in sambar?
The coffee, saved for last,
Not before the penultimate sheera,
Beginning mornings,
Or ending days,
Sometimes even,
At the crack of dawn.

Handwritten Notes

I love handwritten notes.
They could never collate,
To digital messages,
Even if printed on paper.

Those emotions in binary,
Convey better,
When you use your favourite stationery.
Your choicest paper, your favourite pen,
Your words, complemented by doodles,
The ink, bleeding through the pen.

Your handwriting,
Your pace on paper,
Mirroring the heart,
That beats in your chest.

Post-it notes,
You leave on doors.
Scribbles on the napkin,
From our brunches.
Sometimes, when you are in the mood,
Handmade paper is the one you choose.

Important messages,
Reminders,

Quotes you came across,
Sometimes something straightforward,
"Hey, smile when you see this"
At times, long letters,
Explanations,
Revelations,
Elaborations and more.

The Hypocrite

I refuse to accept,
Your love,
Thrown at me like leftovers.
I deserve the gourmet version,
For the love I have always given you.

I refuse to accept,
Your attention, when drifting,
In a thousand different directions,
It's your acknowledgment I seek.

You unsee me,
With a masterful grace and ease,
For my listening ear has heard,
All the words you uttered,
And even those you left unsaid.

You could care about a million things,
And yet you choose to be,
Unbothered about me.

I would want to let you know,
As they say,
We don't value what we have,
Until it is all lost.

Your efforts wasted then,
Why even pretend?
Save that energy for the better.

A pretentious persona,
Gracing you like a showstopper outfit.
Your unbothered mascara,
Your silent lipstick,
Your washed-out jewellery,
Just making some noise.

Your layered coat,
Masking your dimwit.
Your Alpha manliness,
Like cracked glass.

Your ramp walk seems dead,
Just drifting,
I don't even recognize you anymore,
Your body,
Covered in the soot,
Of your burnt being.
And yet,
In my acknowledgement of you,
I say,
Thank You for everything.

That vanished love

It wasn't anything out of the ordinary,
To feel empty.
It had become,
A part of me,
As much as blood cells.
Blood cells,
That formed my being,
Took oxygen,
To parts that lacked more,
Even though I breathed every day,
But was breathing enough to feel alive?

I spent nights,
Reminiscing,
Those mornings spent together,
In your arms,
Where the world felt smaller,
The strange anxiety of tomorrow,
Didn't matter much to me,
With you by my side then.

The moon touched my shoulder,
And,
I longed for a vanished love.

Treading with care

My heart is password-protected,
With two-factor authentication,
Stifling minutes,
Uncertainty, inconsistency,
I am just safeguarding something precious.

Wouldn't call this a trust issue,
It isn't one,
How else would I open up to you?
I am surprised.

Good times,
Bring happiness,
Accompanied by the side effects,
Thinking, how long will this last?
Practicality hitting me,
Do good things last forever?

I have faith in my inner self,
Taking each day as it comes.
I have surrendered to my Shiva,
Guiding me,
My breath moves at his will.

I wait for this haze,
To disappear,

Intentions,
Becoming crystal clear.

Pure hearts,
Never fear the Power.
We are not pretending,
But acting on the script,
Of He who calls the shots.

Beginnings

These words entwined,
Its meaning,
Undefined.
Like sea-waves in a rush,
Feelings bottled up,
Quite crushed.
Two steps I take,
Two steps you do.
Perfect our pace,
Meet at that spot,
Reached by few.
Dreaming now,
Eyes closed tight.
Reality sneaks a peak,
Hoping to get it right.
That tap on the shoulder,
Those fingers,
Holding strong.
That look of assurance.
The journey commencing,
Forever and more.

Footprint Streak

Unlock those secrets,
Unlock those dreams,
Face the mighty,
Silence those screams.
Look at all that's ingrained in the crystal,
Transparent, when hit by the light,
Leaves a splatter,
Thoughts, feelings, and emotions.
Choose the path, that which you deem fit,
Pain and pleasure,
Always exist.
Wipe off that haze,
Settled when floating,
Let your eyes see,
Which the mind knows,
And the heart can give the courage to face.
The scale holders,
Of right and wrong,
Their only job,
Break you while strong.
Give that gut feeling a chance,
Let your heart do one happy dance.
Trekked, once you reach that windy peak,
Leaving to follow the footprint streak.

Mirage

I look far till my vision holds me.
I find a silvery mirage.
I see humans emerge,
From the silvery wave.
The closer they come,
The farther my feet push me.
The mirage stays,
Forever a silvery haze.
I wonder,
Have these gaps reduced?
Having fallen asleep,
In the scorching desert heat,
I wake up to find,
A hand holding out.
Come with me,
He says,
This dust is not your place.
I clear my eyes,
My vision of him,
Blocked by the dust,
And wonder,
If my heart caught some rust.
My feet, like before, refuse to move.
My eyes are moist,
My vision wants more.
I hold on to that hand,

Grab by the wrist.
As the winds run wild,
My heart opens like a child.
Maybe I am finally free,
Trapped all this time,
Even though no barriers exist.
Bounded to someone now,
Still, free to my will.
We ride horseback,
I see the silvery haze,
Moving closer with every stride,
Thoughts racing my mind,
Will I be any different,
Or,
Will the mirage remain the same?

Faraway Bonds

I wish we were all together,
Right now, in the same city.
I wish it was the very same traffic,
That we would complain about,
It was the same weather,
We would love or hate,
It would be the same spots,
That we grew up in,
Where we would hang now,
As 30-somethings,
Cribbing, laughing, and observing them GenZs.

I wish we could catch up,
Every week over dates and sleepovers,
Talk about,
Small meaningless updates and events,
Watch each other grow,
Face challenges and heal together.

I wish we were part of each other's,
New beginnings and chapters that closed.
I wish it was more than just voice notes,
Texts, videos, and calls,
When sometimes a virtual hand reaches out for
help,
I wish we could group hug for real,

Not mentally, most times as we have been doing,
For years now.
I wish we could hold hands,
When our touch reassures us,
More than our words,
That all will be okay,
And this too shall pass.

I know real friendships,
Have always stood the test of time.
I know we are the same,
Even when many seasons have passed,
Between when we last met and now.
Yet I miss you, Dear friend.
Sometimes, you are a drive away,
Sometimes, I would have to cross oceans,
And sometimes,
Even a trip around the sun wouldn't bring you
back,
Cause you have passed on to a better world.

If you are reading this here,
I want to tell you,
That I love you,
And I miss you.
Not just when I tell you that I do,
But even when I have not.

Here's to my ancestors

Here's to my ancestors,
You made do with very little yourselves,
Strived and struggled,
Created diamonds from dust,
Survived under pressure,
You lived like that,
So that,
We could live,
The way we do right now.

You saw wars,
Survived them,
You saw the Crown fall,
And,
Democracy taking birth,
You saw a different India,
You watched the world transform,
Unlike any other,
Slowly,
Yet,
Seeming very fast,
In retrospect.
You saw time move differently,
Over all these years.

I can say,

When I think about you,
That you loved differently.
You loved patiently,
You loved with care,
And regard,
You did not know any different.
You could easily forgive.

Here's to my ancestors,
Because,
You accepted us.
You saw us grow up,
In a world,
Very different from yours.
We were, at times,
Faster.
Faster at decisions,
Faster at inhibitions,
Faster at feeling sad.
Slower.
Slower at patience,
Slower at loving,
Slower at being happy,
Yet,
You embraced us.

You leave behind lessons.
You leave behind a history,
We can call ours.

One that we revisit,
In your stories,
In your memories,
In those places,
That still reminds us of You.

Thoughts

Thoughts last for a lifetime,
Thoughts can never die.
Thoughts are not vulnerable,
Thoughts do not cry.
Thoughts are the lights,
In a dark room.
Thoughts are the drops,
In the ocean of life.
Thoughts come, and thoughts go,
Although never out of your mind.
Thoughts can fade away in the darkness,
And come back through light.
Thoughts reside in the mind,
Not in the heart,
Where they are difficult to find.
What would have been life,
Without a thought?
As a thought can,
Change a life.
Thoughts are just,
Reflections of honesty,
As thoughts do not disguise.
Thoughts would have never thought,
To think what thoughts could do!
Thoughts can do wonders.
You would have,

Thought that too.

Dream Castle Block

Walking over,
That cobbled street,
Hands dusty,
And untidy feet.
Sparkling eyes,
Hands, holding those rusting keys.
A dainty persona,
Yet a gait of strength.
She walked,
Up the road,
To the Dream Castle block.

Peeping Tom's and Tiffany's,
All watched her,
With their closed minds.
Their glaring looks,
Pushing her down,
That guilt-stricken drain.
Spotting, she skipped,
And to herself,
She quipped,
You can't make me fall.

For I may trip,
I may stall,
But I shall reach,
The Dream Castle Block.

The long walk up,
Followed by an army,
That stalks,
She reached,
Those rusted gates.
As her fingers,
Touched the red metal,
Specks of gold dust,
On it so settled.
Her eyes, luminescent,
And mouth open wide,
The army behind,
In amazement,
Cried!

The doors opened,
A carpet of thorns,
Lay strewn,
With rose petals just born.
As she stepped on them,
Her feet, unacquainted with such softness,
Midway stopped.
Before she could lay down her heel,
She sat down in a kneel,
And shed a tear of joy.
She was finally here,
And this near.

The army now,
Behind her back,
Becoming her strength,
Lifted her,
Walking towards her throne.
The mirrored walls,
Reflected on the bright future,
That lay ahead.

As she accessioned,
With those dainty feet,
A white light,
From the heavens fell,
A proclamation made,
The curse now lifted its veil.
Her crown arrived,
And every second,
Passed, like a year.
For a brief moment in time,
Everything had just stopped.
Her soul swam in glory,
And a destiny, a fate,
Turned, so rightfully hers!

Whispers from my Desk

Waking up to that sound,
Of rain drops around,
A morning like this,
An absolute bliss.

Effort you take,
To get out of bed,
The outside, so pleasant,
Yet it's a Monday you dread!

That morning cup, brewing,
More thoughts over coffee beans,
Yet the aroma kicks in stronger,
While watching, raindrops splash on glass
screens.

This time calls for a walk,
With a loved one in tow,
With an umbrella that does no good,
And yet, would not have been better.

Instead,
You bring your mind,
Within the confines of those brick walls,
Suit up now and take that bow!
While walking you wonder,

Why the clouds in this sky,
Oh, so thunder!
The puddles, and potholes,
The construction sites,
The trek through canyons, craters, and more.

While you aim to reach,
In a presentable piece.
Soggy feet and wet hair,
That's none that you care.

Ting-Ting goes your phone,
Like launched drones.
This day's beauty enjoyed,
Just in fleeting thoughts,
Accommodating we become,
And our feelings fought!

The smell of wet soil,
That chattering of birds,
Impending assignments,
Meetings that lurk!

It's just the beginning,
Of days filled with rain,
Get used to it,
There's more, aplenty,
From which you can't refrain.

Ocean

Magnificent,
Raging with gigantic waves and tides,
Weaving brave sagas of wars and conquests,
Having travelled across continents,
Creating a world of its own.

Soothing,
Serene and still with sunlight glimmering,
Shining like blue sapphire entwined in gold,
The winds,
Blowing just right.
Guiding through struggles,
And phases of Calm.

Protecting,
Blanketing three worlds,
Above, beneath and beyond,
A blast of colours beneath,
Life nurtured for thousands of years,
Your beauty from above,
Most perceived.
Beyond is unknown.

Mysterious,
Hiding creatures, cities, souls, and more,
Secrets waiting to be revealed,
Or stay hidden just as before.

Struggling,
Gasping for oxygen,
Gasping for life,
While you give us ours,
Drowning within yourself,
Belittled by an army of nomads,
Failing to understand your power.

Earth's Witness

The blue sky,
Looking beneath,
Finds a hoard,
Crying deep.
It wonders,
How these years have passed,
Fighting, igniting, complaining,
Loving and hating,
Of all the tribes amassed.

The sky screams,
Our naivety exposed,
As beautiful years,
Wasted, equated to dust.
Stuck up in messes,
Ones before us created,
Have we learned from our past?

The time is now,
An awakening, calls.
Nature could soon,
Take its toll.

This battle would not be,
An easy one.
Predictions and strategies,

We pray work.

Fight through words,
Through actions,
Let them be our Arsenal.
Mother Nature calls out,
Fight for that,
Which makes our world,
A safer Home.

Dear Poet

As poets,
We express a spectrum of emotions.
We lead our minds,
Onto treks.
Sometimes surrounded,
Of nature's beauty,
Sometimes,
Facing its wrath.
We deal with negativity,
Through our words,
Often giving us a catharsis,
Expressed in rhymes.
I tell you, Dear poet,
Allow yourself to feel,
Hurt, anger, jealousy,
Distraught and any heart-breaking emotion,
You could think.
But don't you dare lose Hope!
Hope is the seedling that keeps life going,
Water your Hope with love,
It may seem scarce,
But there's enough around.
And if ever you feel low,
A cataract of the soul,
Blurring out possibilities in store,
Come back to my poem.

This one is for you.

Release

Close your eyes,
Do you hear,
There is chaos around?
Most times,
You would hear it,
The loudest,
In moments of Silence,
Filled with unspoken words,
Parked thoughts,
You are too afraid to think,
Drifting through the air,
Unacknowledged for long.
Stand still now,
And wait.
You may get pushed about,
Through limiting beliefs,
Ingrained in your subconscious.
Fictional stories,
Fictional perceptions of you,
Others created,
Which you started believing,
Factually yours.

Listen to your heart,
A voice is calling you out,
Unearth that sound,

Buried deep.
It isn't you,
That which you are trying to be.
Step into the light,
Let everyone come and see.
Embrace your authentic,
Embrace your truth,
Embrace the child,
Who wasn't wise enough then,
To choose.
For pretending is playing,
With God's own choice,
Unleash the purest,
You were born to be.

Surface Perception

For you see flaws,
In glass-covered eyes,
That have dreams,
Reaching far beyond the skies.

For you see flaws,
On my skin,
I would choose more of this,
Than I have ever been.

For you see flaws,
In the words I utter,
Too audacious for you,
Which leaves you to mutter.

For you see flaws,
In feet daring to run wild,
Your own slow pace,
Your mind is a shackled case.

For you see flaws,
In my hands writing,
My destiny,
My fate, with your plans fighting.

For you see flaws,
In my optimism, my thoughts,
Taking birth by,
Facing challenges brought.

For you see flaws,
In my ambition to succeed,
Causing your own,
Failures to breed.

For you see flaws,
In my heart's ability to love,
Wrapped inside you in a quilt,
Your dishonesty, your guilt, like a caged dove.

Unconditional Love

Where expectations cease,
Where feelings freeze,
Where wishes are pure,
Where the heart meets its cure,
Unconditional love unveils,
Like a diamond from coal.
Where life meets,
The reason to live,
Where your palms open,
Only to give,
Protect this love,
Whilst you receive.
Send it out,
From your heart's core.

The Trespasser

She had never seen him,
They had not yet met.
Those conversations belonged,
To both of them.
His prompts made her dive,
Into the deepest trenches of her heart,
A narration encompassing decades,
Summarised in words,
She carefully chose.
There isn't much one can convey,
In fleeting moments,
And yet those brief calls,
Brought out exactly,
The parts he wanted to hear,
And the ones she always wanted to tell.
His listening ear,
Filled up the void.
The void had made all those stories,
Hidden, in mysterious caves of her being.
He was the trespasser,
Her scared self embraced.

Tipping Point

The older they got,
It was clearer to them,
As to why they fought,
Why they screamed,
Why love at home was not the one,
Portrayed in movies and stories,
They realized,
They were children,
From broken mansions,
And they,
Searched for shelters,
And not homes.

It reflected on who they loved,
And how they loved them,
Unfortunately misunderstood,
Always ending up,
Solving puzzles in human form.
Their subconscious,
Trying to find the last puzzle,
That could fit.
But never complete their own.

They carried scars,
Unhealed from their past.
Now,

Addicted to the pain it brought.
If only they could see,
Their cure,
Lay in just being,
With each other,
Holding hands,
Through those haunted trails,
One of them had walked before.

It was easier,
To brush their issues,
Under the carpets,
To the point,
They would trip,
Frequently over the piles formed.
And when they fell,
I hope it wasn't too late.

Too late,
To start over.
Too late,
To forgive.
Too late,
To find the reason.
Too late,
To being locked up,
In a room,
With missing pieces,
Of their unsolved puzzles.

Her Strong

Many conflicts she didn't sign up for,
And battles lost,
But rising from every fall,
Had made her strong.

Many idols worshipped,
Some prayers remain unanswered,
Having an undying faith,
Had made her strong.

Many opportunities she missed,
Many stones upon which she tripped,
Getting up and dusting away the dust,
Had made her strong.

Putting the bad behind her,
And, taking the good forward,
Conquering hearts,
Winning smiles,
On her way to a new world,
Had made her strong.

Black, White and Grey

A blank space,
A patch of black,
White spots,
Make a stack.
Out they spread untypically,
Scattered, yet meaning all the same.
Drops of white,
In a lake all black,
Scattered, for now,
Combined soon when they meet.
The patterns change,
No more they remain,
White blobs of paint,
But a river of grey.
Conscience, if ever,
Were to dip in that river,
Shall grey more than ever.
We are all,
A patch of black,
With blobs of white.
Who decides,
That means black,
Who decides,
That means white,
And who shall ever,
Explain what's grey.

There is beauty in all three,
So is deception.
We are all in between,
Rarely, at one spectrum.
We are all the same,
Yet so different.

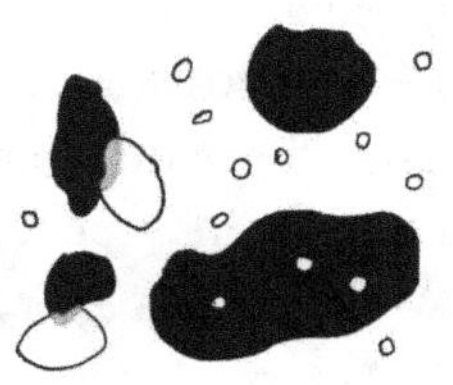

Change

As these winds pass by,
I think to myself,
And don't deny,
Change occurs,
Despite resistance,
Transformation happens,
On your insistence.
A new lesson every day,
Chapters written,
As myself-watches from the bay.
My heart feels new pain,
Yet every touch is a healing gain.
Isn't this how life intends to be?
Hazes our vision,
Giving us the knowledge to see.

When He Knew

He knew it was love,
When even in a room full of people,
He could only see her!

He knew it was love,
When all the sounds in the air,
Mellowed for him,
To hear his beats,
Loud and clear.

He knew it was love,
When even her silence,
Was music to his ears.

He knew it was love,
When she chose him,
To bear witness to her,
Innermost fears.

He knew it was love,
When he envisioned,
A future with her.

He knew it was love,
When her last call,
Was his lullaby.

He knew it was love,
When her pain,
Gave him,
Sleepless nights.

He knew it was love,
When her hand,
Was his anchor,
Holding his ground.

He knew it was love,
When her victories,
Crowned him like,
A King.

He knew it was love,
When he broke shackles,
Binding him for her.

He knew it was love,
When he put her needs,
In front of his own.

He knew it was love,
When she became,
A constant,
In his prayers.

He knew it was love,
When he recognized,
Her inner divine,
And his inner divine,
Worshipped hers.

Holding On

Why do we hurt?
Why is there pain and sorrow?
Why?
For no reason at all?
Does our heart,
Tears, it borrows?
The colours of these rainbows,
Turning pastel,
The dimming lights,
Spreading gloom.
I look at that face,
Cheeks left salty,
Eyes turned pink,
A smile, now faulty.
What is said,
Is now told,
What's now done,
Will not be undone.
With every gust of wind,
Her pieces fly away.
So tiny, they seem,
Do not gather if scattered away.
She sits stuck,
Failing to move.
Slowly, the parts of her,
Leaving,

Deceiving,
Her willpower.
She searches for light,
At the end of the tunnel.
The silver lining,
On the grey cloud.
This vision blurred,
Shall her hope escape away?
And then comes her saviour,
A saviour called Time.
His presence, so vast,
Nothing escapes from his glance.
His biggest lesson,
'This too shall pass.'
The light she searched,
Glistening in the black of her eyes,
Her tears,
Turning sweet from salty.
These are the ones,
She happily cries.

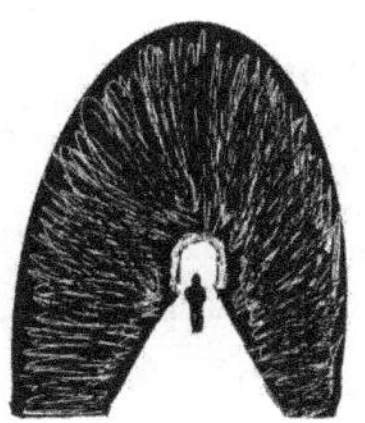

The Terminal

Our time here,
Is limited,
We come with a two-way ticket.
A part of our journey,
Completes at birth,
The life,
Is our wait,
At the terminal.
An unknown boarding time,
For our way back to beyond,
Not accounting, the time we waste,
On anger,
Guilt,
And jealousy,
To name a few.
Punishing ourselves,
And the ones we love,
For our inadequacies.
Sometimes,
Our inability,
To handle the truth,
To accept things,
As they are,
Leading us on a path,
Of self-destruction.
Even though,

We come here alone,
And shall go back,
Alone,
We are tied,
To people.
If we could be,
Solitary bodies in space,
This world,
Probably,
A better place.
Peaceful,
Yet gloomy,
With no interactions.
Lessons we ought to learn,
Come to us when,
We forgive.
Grudges turning into,
Acid for our soul.
Forgetting that,
Karma takes care of everything.
If we knew,
How long shall we last,
We could be happier,
Realising the value,
Of making someone smile,
Of loving someone unconditionally,
Of setting goals,
Achieving them well in time.
Since we don't know,

When we shall bid adieu,
To all the things,
That keeps us attached,
Bounded,
And grounded,
There is just one way,
To go on every day.
Counting each day to be your last.
Spending it in gratitude,
For the love,
Received from all those that matter.
Do it every day!
Feeling shy,
To say I love you,
To express our deepest feelings,
We have nothing to lose.
The last minute I spend,
Could never be in regret.
Remember,
Only those relationships matter,
That lets you grow,
Make you better,
And that has your back.
Doesn't matter,
How many people are there in your life,
What matters is,
Having people sincerely love you.
Buddha said,
The root of all causes is attachment,

If we can free ourselves,
If we can try,
To be as much of a solitary body,
As we can be in this life,
We can hope,
For a better wait at the terminal.

77

Moment

Stop right there,
Look around,
Let's not care,
Kneel to the ground.

Close your eyes,
Take that deep breath,
Forget the time spies,
Feel the happiness stretch.

There are greens and blues,
And all sorts of hues,
Blossoming, fragrant flowers,
In the haze of the present.

The clouds escaping,
Your window's view.
Mental pictures,
On the leaves catching dew.

An Ode to Our Bravehearts

Heavy heart and heavy sighs,
As we wake up to these cries,
Unstoppable moist eyes,
Lake of hope that never dries,
Burnt to ashes,
Lifted to the skies,
These mighty Bravehearts,
Bidding us a goodbye.
With one passing by,
Hundreds more become alive,
It's a fight we cannot deny.
Silence makers with loud thuds,
Wish to crush our hearts,
The soul within is unbreakable,
Housing a million iron darts,
Each pointing now to,
Peace-breakers,
Trouble-makers,
Life-takers,
This shall not go on.
These invaders do not belong,
Our land,
Our mother,
For her, we do not deter,
Before rose petals on those caskets wither,
Before the flames on the candles start to flicker,

Answer in harmony, answer in might,
Answer in black,
Answer in white.
The mettled fence with currents running
through,
Separates the soil,
From which they both grew,
Brothers then of the same Motherland,
Fed and nourished by the very same hand,
United we stood, modest and content,
Divided we fell, promising lives to defend.

The Climb

They had walked,
Far, through slow breezes,
Turning into roaring winds.
Hand in hand.
His trembling in hers,
And hers in his.

It was a long trek,
Through those trails,
When she brought,
His hand,
Closer to her lips,
And blew a kiss.

Landing at the foothills,
An even tougher climb,
Awaited.
This was uphill.

Walking against,
Gravity,
Perceptions,
Fears,
Biased opinions,
Pulling them down,
Their uphill climb,

Though,
Still hand in hand.
She was his anchor,
And he,
Hers.

As the crescent moon's,
Eyes smiled,
Looking down on them,
Gravity,
Turned into the strongest force,
Love.
This mountain tip,
Awaited them.
It was where the brightest specks,
Of stardust fell.

And as their eyes met,
They saw a reflection,
Of care,
Of love,
Of happiness,
Once which they held within,
For themselves,
Now,
In equal measure,
For each other.

Flow

It was as if Time,
Would wait,
Patiently in his honor.
Every millisecond,
It felt like a second,
And a second,
It felt like an hour,
So that he could,
Look into her eyes,
And see the lifetimes,
They would spend together.

Echoes beyond the page

A Dictionary,
Explaining every word known,
I wonder,
How it defines emotions,
In pages,
With meaning and sentences for context.
Anger,
Disgust,
Shame,
Fear,
Happiness,
Sadness,
Surprise, love, and more,
Even in an infinity's measure,
We can't fathom the essence,
Of a feeling,
Just, about easily composed,
In a word of four alphabets,
LOVE.
Can it be explained?
With just a bunch of words,
And punctuation.
It takes a gamut of experiences,
Number of years,
And,
Sometimes milliseconds,

To comprehend deep complexities,
Understanding nuances,
Of emotions,
That makes the entire,
Human experience.

Mending

The selfish became,
The most generous,
In teaching lessons.

The craters they formed,
Now overflowed,
Of emptiness.
Her prayers played on deaf ears,
They could not listen to her silence.

Letting them go,
Became the easiest part,
Of her misery.
The toughest,
Was to revive,
Her erased being.

While she repaired the craters,
From sources of Love,
That never had its dearth,
She realized,
That it was pain,
That was difficult to forget,
And Love,
Difficult to remember.

Time

We are trapped,
Most certainly in Time,
Even though it's infinite.

www.ingramcontent.com/pod-product-compliance
Lightning Source LLC
LaVergne TN
LVHW011039200726
843509LV00011B/1313